YOU COULD NEVER OBJECTIFY ME MORE THAN I'VE ALREADY OBJECTIFIED MYSELF

ALEXANDRA NAUGHTON

PUNK♥HOSTAGE♥PRESS

**YOU COULD NEVER OBJECTIFY ME MORE THAN
I'VE ALREADY OBJECTIFIED MYSELF**
ALEXANDRA NAUGHTON

©Alexandra Naughton

ISBN-10: 1940213800
ISBN-13: 978-1-940213-80-4

All rights reserved. Printed in the United States of America. No part of this text may be used or reproduced in any manner whatsoever without written permission from the author or publisher except in case of brief quotations embodied in critical articles and reviews. For more information contact:

Punk Hostage Press
P.O. Box 1869
Hollywood CA 90078
www.punkhostagepress.com

Editor: A. Razor

Cover Design: Geoff Melville, A. Razor

Author photo: Joe Carrow

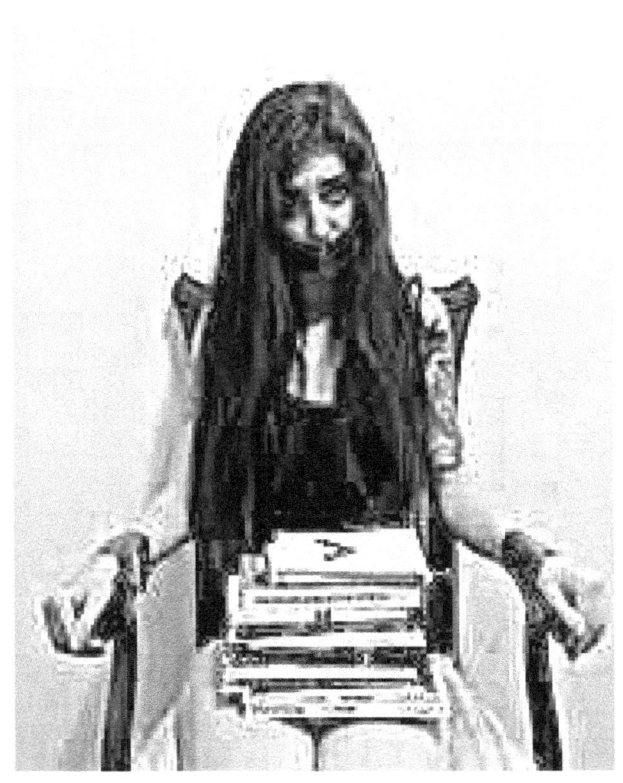

hello I am a quirky girl artist person and I am here to teach you a lesson about yourself. it is my true purpose. I don't exist except for you.

getting myself off thinking about you dreaming about me
I posted that on tumblr

fifteen minutes later my only fan texted me

'I jerked off to your photo on HTMLgiant'

I am an alt lit superstar.

...this is how it starts like watching your skin tighten and relax when you realize it like the blood under the pores that gets so hot and sticky you can feel it seeping slowly out like the dirt that collects under remorseful fingernails

or did I skip ahead

maybe it starts in the middle or closer to the end after the worst of it when you're left with heat damaged plastic containers and dollar store trashbags to pack your life in after your friends have already given up on you after you've waited so long to eat you're no longer hungry but you take small bites of a premade sandwich because you know you should have something

but how does it really start does it start in the beginning like being spoken to in the ear you can only kind of hear out of and nodding like knowing you're about to fail again but it's never the beginning because you're never ready because you never finish anything it's all a continuous failure and you ease in and let it happen a pretty young some would say attractive some would say fuckable some would say a lot of things but this is not the point it is only to establish a theme.

I think instead of texting you I'm just going to write in my notebook what I wanted to text you

/////////////////////////////////oh goddddddddddddddddddddddddddddddddddddd dddddddddddddddddddddddddddddddddddddddd ddddd;;
..........,.,.,.,.,,,,,,,,,
,,,,,,,,,,,, , , , ,

dirty like my hair, tangle tangle tangle

I want to make myself almost vulnerable in front of you compulsively, obsessively

smell this affliction
witness these bruises
put your face in this longing

I want you to be just as tortured, and singularly
your thinking should be mine
tattoo my tear stains on your belly
lol, I am so possessive

burn your words at my heel one letter at a time

she wants the help, but won't settle for feature, sideshow. scratching for bylines and passing gingerly over collected bodies, disfigured, wet with crumpled sugar, mystery boxes at auction.

not aspire to be tangible fruit, a game that sells, aesthetically inferior. a soft individual, picking tropes. there to assist. the only purpose is be sweet, to assist.

It's happening all over again where the bridge looks like a dinosaur skeleton and I miss you. How is that even possible like just writing to you and wanting to bile out. Wanting to bileout. Wantingtobileout. Bile the fuck out. How many times will I write this poem. Digging fingernails into palm until warm crust appears and I feel something else. This is what happens when you chincheck ghosts.

They don't hit back but it hurts as much, stinging your teeth.

why why why why am I not so inquisitive always
throwing myself at conclusions slutty for
nonsense so thirsty in the grill and just wanting
it to stop even if a minute later I had just asked
why why why but you're shit and I'm shit so I
just say you be right you be right you be right
you be right

I want to ask I don't want to ask but I want to tell
I don't want to tell I need to show you I don't
need to do anything

life is really just a series of pressures in which
to embarrass oneself

I make my bones exposing my parts
making bones
nothing to achieve from holding
little to sully from embracing
some apologist's respect

I am trained for this
I am made for this
I am made for this
I have made this
I have it harnessed so sexy

I can't make my mind. Yours or anyones. And likewise. That's the beauty of it.

motoring in and out of dreams
driving up the spines of bridges and losing
souvenirs, my stockings, senses momentarily
cruising on foot on eroded sidewalks jabbing at
leftovers left to find a textbook, grieving card,
grunt of disapproval, something to take with me
to make a memory
keep as a reminder
everything is worth saving

I keep a face like public transit

I make time counting telephone poles

the autumn of my disaffection falls over your
shoulders imagining me mounting you

I misread your words but prefer my version

I am that parted mouth maximized on your screen

I am that soft pixelated burn you carry with you

you want me because you don't know me

you don't want me to know too much

I am whatever you want me to be in your mind

I am whatever you want except what I am

Oh god why I always do like torturing. But validated. In a sensitive way. I don't need it to survive. If you're going to occupy. Feel a similar impact because what's the point. My affections are capitalist. It's almost like I have decent handwriting. I guess I am calm. Maybe not I have terrible handwriting haha I write that in a letter to you or you write that in yours. So self conscious. Or maybe it's just me. Keep pressing that little button. Talk about writing. We're always talking about writing it's the only way we can talk about fucking.

Bus riding garbage arms of clothes up steep streets leaning forward to stay balanced keep everything from falling out. Feeling like falling out of my body. Falling out of this plane onto another plane. Falling into something comforting in a grimy way. Comforting like anyone.

I don't need you to say anything I just want to say it to you to kill it you don't even have to look at me. So many questions I want to say but don't want to know the answers to. Some time like at my desk or in my bed with my cat. Jesus Christ in a near catatonic state like that hot tub scene in Ferris Bueller just staring at some odd point on the wall like a picture of Al Pacino or the bottom blind in the row and I wish I had a plan.

Bathroommouth open and grimace and notice something in my teeth the pair of old underwear from the trash more holes than blood stains. I think as an animal swimming or bobbing up and down while trying to catch the surface of a wave but maybe I'm just a large rock the water splashes over.

I see the commuter train coming quick and remember passing Carlotta street calling it in my head mad Carlotta street. Mad Carlotta, mad Carlotta, she used to be sad Carlotta, she used to be Carlotta the beautiful, Carlotta the debutante, but now she's just mad mad mad Carlotta. Almost perfectly walk toward the tracks put out a cigarette how if the train had caught me you might remember me.

Manic pixie dream girl. Manic pixelated dream girl. Manic pixie mean girl. Manic pixie C.R.E.A.M. girl. Manic pixie I'm not your girl. Manic pixie ice queen. Manic pixie drama queen. Manic pixie queen bee. Manic pixie colony collapse disorder. Manic pixie break down. Manic pixie depressive disorder. Manic pixie you don't really know me.

Manic pixie scream girl. Manic pixie no one's dream girl. Manic pixie don't pin me down girl. Manic pixie everybody's it girl. Manic pixie I'm the shit girl. Manic pixie male protagonist and the real girl. Manic pixie am I real girl.

We don't have capitalism we have corporate fascism.

I am a capitalist body.

I can bring value to a product.

My art becomes a product once I remove it from myself.

Watch me remove it from myself and pay me for the spectacle

It all sucks, so make more //////   /////////////
/ / / / /   /------ //////////
coded but expository all
//
////////////thesame.

You're

_____
_____   too
much   here.

Make it hurt like a sneeze su
ppressed.   Choking
like a
                                        fuckboi's
touch.

Revealing as a whimper.

Ugly like a
      knife.

Pretty like a
      knife.

not like seeking like
surface seeking surface
shades seeking worth

hate recognize hate
wraith recognize wraith

decay is just another form of force

do you see me being
could you even

we can't ever know
everyone is gossiping

you want me to be less eager
you want a girl feminine and waiting
you want someone to give permission
you want to make an escape
you want me to know already
you want to not know the details
you want to illustrate it yourself
you want to pantomime the weather
you want to color the insides
you want to play the timeline out

I love you like every poem I ever forgot
like every line I didn't write down
like every word I mispronounced

I love you like the ashes on my pillow
like the yellowing of my teeth
like the way you can see the enamel splinter

I love you like every gift I ever gave away
like the screenprint t-shirt my dad made I let my high-school boyfriend borrow
like my first skateboard I bought with water ice money I gave my cough syrup friend

I love you like every function I everwithered
like every anxiety assisted hesitation
like every chance I never took

I love you like every deleted message
like every rumor I wanted to spread and didn't
like every time I swallowed a hurt

I love you like every frenemy I acknowledge
like every thank you note I carelessly sent
like every smile I am afraid to return

I love you like every fleeting shadow on my

shoulder
like every lingering mumble
like every cold hand in my sheets

I love you like a memory I never had
like a dream I can only see pieces of
like a ghost I thought I saw in the mirror

like loving a ghost
like loving a grave

like a lost sock you will never see again
even if you know its resting place

like you never knew it
like you wanted to know it
like you only knew about it when it was too late

like it was never going to go the way you
wanted

like you knew the whole time but couldn't help
prodding

like it was always impossible
like even if the timing was different

like you didn't care if it could ever be right
like you love feeling lousy with curses

like the guilt gets you off

like you don't know how else to feel
like you don't have feelings

like it could have never mattered
like it didn't matter anyway

manic pixie break down manic pixie break down
manic pixie break down and Lindsay Lohan
looks happy and healthy on the red carpet in
Austria

in every dream home a heartache in every
dream girl in every dream girl is a Brittany
Murphy who may have been exposed to tainted
drugs ...

dream girl heartache manic pixie break down
dream girl heartache dream girl heartache
dream girl heartache I told you not to call me
dream girl, I am not your dream girl

manic pixie break down in a dream home
having heart aches like Britney Spears
'relapsed' on drugs and spent the night in her
car during meltdown

broken dream girl broken heart aches dreams
of girls breaking hearts and breaking down
everything obligated to leave, obligated to stay,
obligated to always keep track of paces I don't
want to be scared into doing things

but don't you get it
the silences is part of the poem too
it's everything I could say
but won't

feeling like a placeholder like a scratch paper
bookmark keeping your spot for when you
decide to pick up your life

I don't want to be your manic pixie dream girl or otherwise
I don't want you to like my writing because you want to fuck me

I want you to want to fuck me because you like my writing

I'm thinking a lot about being a girl on the internet and honestly it's breaking me
this cult of online personalities all so carefully manicured / curated
thinking what it means when a stranger says I'm their muse
thinking what it means when a stranger tells me when they jerk off to my profile photos

identity as masturbation fantasy

what is the point of sharing intimacies with someone who will cash out suddenly
what is the sense
what purpose did I serve
it is not important
but why would you think I could serve a purpose at all
and why would I be complicit

I want to lay on a flaming pond
I want to watch myself luxuriate, entombed

He was like, no, that's not how you cut out a snowflake. Stop doing it that way.

And you were like, do you think people would take me more seriously if I started to braid my hair.

Then I was like, this. This is why I stopped reading the news. And, where did my cat go.

Then someone behind us shouted, look up! And we did and the moon was enormous.

I don't want to be one note I want to be discordant. I posted that on facebook. It got maybe 18 likes. My average is 30. More if it's a photo. I still liked it enough to try to make a poem out of it.

I want to lay on a flaming pond.

I want to watch myself luxuriate, entombed.

I don't want to be one note I want to be discordant.

Nobody is just one thing. We are composed of the things that have happened
to us and how we happened to them. How we remember them without regulation.
Nothing is homogenous, even when processed.

I wish I didn't see some of the things that I do see but if I didn't who would

I don't want to save you
I don't want to save anyone
on this tenderoni schtick

I'm not a savior
no one is
not even internetselfhelpgurus

we pass empathies like needles

I don't want to fix you
or anyone
I don't think I can fix anything

you will you can you want

want more than need

I don't want to write false posi poetry
I don't even believe in a lot of things
I think I can believe in a person
or maybe just the idealized

it's never the one I want

I want to twist cliched disasters into something
we can taste and feel and fuck with

my dreams are like horror stories that I read
and forget the endings to

Your eyes conform the image. You make the image what you want.

All that matters is your imagination. Anoint the image with alkaline.

I have hands and feet. I think. I have quirks and twerks. You think.

Overdosing on filthy puzzles. No wonder there is no room left.

we agree on everything and we don't
understand each other

I like your expectations so I know when you're disappointing me. You said we were like John and Yoko and you were right.

It wasn't about me. It never was. I was sometimes the escape, an escape like a chore, like a detour, but never the reason. An ever reason but not me, too much too much. Sometimes the excuse but never the answer, never the answer, because who could ever know, and you don't want me to.

I will let it melt. I will let it smirk through my fingers and under my nails.

Would I.

I could have helped. I could have never helped.

Photo by Alexandra Naughton

Alexandra Naughton might be here or probably not and can't decide which is better. She is known for *I Will Always Be Your Whore/Love Songs for Billy Corgan* published by Punk Hostage Press, 2013. Her other titles include *I Will Always Be In Love* (Dig That Book Co., 2015), *My Posey Taste Like* (Bottlecap Press, 2015), and tsaritsa of the wired.

"Alexandra Naughton's work here balances both straightforward and fragmented expressions of longing, identity, violence, and what it means to be a "woman writer" and a woman human being- all while retaining a powerfully emotional core. It's like reading someone's unfiltered thoughts and feelings, except actually interesting. "
-- Joshua Jennifer Espinoza, author of I'M ALIVE / IT HURTS / I LOVE IT

"Alexandra Naughton's poetry cuts down to the bone, helping to reveal the fact that beyond all else, we are human, looking to feel something that hasn't been compartmentalized by the pop culture that feeds on us as much as we feed on it. These lines are razors, reminiscent of the renegade spirit many of us lost along the way."
--Michael J Seidlinger, author of The Strangest

"'you can never objectify me more than i've already objectified myself' is a manual on how to build and break down heart, detailing inner mechanisms and outer appearances. hold this book in your hands like a still beating organ. you have objectified alexandra naughton, an author who exposes the parts within her that cant be seen. what you have here is not her, but her art. she provides us with it then stands alongside to objectify with us. but screens are shallow surfaces. open this book to sink deeper into your own submission. focus on the way naughton shapes words instead of her self. negative space,

apparent like silence from an upset lover, is where she is left and it's all your fault. from this perspective naughton creates a new heart to objectify. see it for what it isn't, or finally see her for what she is - an artist with a vantage point too high for others to define."
-- ctch bsnss, editor of Similar Peaks

OTHER PUNK HOSTAGE PRESS BOOKS

FRACTURED (2012) by Danny Baker

BETTER THAN A GUN IN A KNIFE FIGHT (2012) by A. Razor

THE DAUGHTERS OF BASTARDS (2012) by Iris Berry

DRAWN BLOOD: COLLECTED WORKS FROM D.B.P.LTD., 1985-1995 (2012) by A. Razor

IMPRESS (2012) by C.V.Auchterlonie

TOMORROW, YVONNE - POETRY & PROSE FOR SUICIDAL EGOISTS (2012) by Yvonne De la Vega

BEATEN UP BEATEN DOWN (2012) by A. Razor

MIRACLES OF THE BLOG: A SERIES (2012) by Carolyn Srygley-Moore

8TH & AGONY (2012) by Rich Ferguson

SMALL CATASTROPHES IN A BIG WORLD (2012) by A. Razor

UNTAMED (2013) by Jack Grisham

MOTH WING TEA (2013) by Dennis Cruz

HALF-CENTURY STATUS (2013) by A. Razor

SHOWGIRL CONFIDENTIAL (2013) by Pleasant Gehman

BLOOD MUSIC (2013) by Frank Reardon

I WILL ALWAYS BE YOUR WHORE/LOVE SONGS for Billy Corgan (2014) by Alexandra Naughton

HISTORY OF BROKEN LOVE THINGS (2014) by SB Stokes

YEAH, WELL... (2014) by Joel Landmine

DREAMS GONE MAD WITH HOPE (2014) by S.A. Griffin

CODE BLUE: A LOVE STORY (2014) by Jack Grisham

HOW TO TAKE A BULLET AND OTHER SURVIVAL POEMS (2014) by Hollie Hardy

DEAD LIONS (2014) by A.D. Winans

SCARS (2014) by Nadia Bruce-Rawlings

STEALING THE MIDNIGHT FROM A HANDFUL OF DAYS (2014) by Michele McDannold

WHEN I WAS A DYNAMITER, Or, How a Nice Catholic Boy Became a Merry Prankster, a Pornographer, and a Bridegroom Seven Times (2104) by Lee Quarnstrom

THUGSNESS AS A VIRTUE (2014) by Hannah Wehr

DAYS OF XMAS POEMS (2014) by A. Razor

FORTHCOMING BOOKS ON PUNK HOSTAGE PRESS

INTROVERT/EXTROVERT (2015) by Russell Jaffe

NO GREATER LOVE (2015) by Die Dragonetti

NO PARACHUTES TO CARRY ME HOME(2015)
by Maisha Z Johnson

L.A. RIVER LULLABY (2015) by Iris Berry

LONGWINDED TALES OF A LOW PLAINS DRIFTER (2015)
by A. Razor

EVERYTHING IS RADIANT BETWEEN THE HATES (2015)
by Rich Ferguson

RAISED BYCRIMINALS, FATHERED BY GONIFFS (2015) by Michael Marcus

GOOD GIRLS GO TO HEAVEN, BAD GIRLS GO EVERYWHERE (2015) by Pleasant Gehman

DANGEROUS INTERSECTIONS (2015) by Annette Cruz

RAW (2015) by Cassandra Dallet

DRIVING ALL OF THE HORSES AT ONCE (2015) by Richard Modiano

NO APOLOGIES (2015) by Jessica Wilson

THE BEAST IS WE (2015) by Dennis Cruz

DISGRACELAND (2015) by Iris Berry & Pleasant Gehman

AND THEN THE ACID KICKED IN (2015) by Carlye Archibeque

BODIES: BRILLIANT SHAPES (2015) by Kate Menzies

BORROWING SUGAR (2015) by Susan Hayden

BASTARD SONS OF ALPHABET CITY (2015) by Jon Hess

THE REDHOOK GIRAFFE & OTHER BROOKLYN TALES (2015) by James A. Tropeano III

PURO PURISMO (2015) by A. Razor

IN THE SHADOW OF THE HOLLYWOOD SIGN (2015) by Iris Berry

www.ingramcontent.com/pod-product-compliance
Lightning Source LLC
Chambersburg PA
CBHW022109040426
42451CB00007B/194